Dear Parent:
Your child's love of read

Every child learns to read in a different way and at his or her own speed. You can help your young reader improve and become more confident by encouraging his or her own interests and abilities. You can also guide your child's spiritual development by reading stories with biblical values and Bible stories, like I Can Read! books published by Zonderkidz. From books your child reads with you to the first books he or she reads alone, there are I Can Read! books for every stage of reading:

SHARED READING
Basic language, word repetition, and whimsical illustrations, ideal for sharing with your emergent reader.

BEGINNING READING
Short sentences, familiar words, and simple concepts for children eager to read on their own.

READING WITH HELP
Engaging stories, longer sentences, and language play for developing readers.

READING ALONE
Complex plots, challenging vocabulary, and high-interest topics for the independent reader.

ADVANCED READING
Short paragraphs, chapters, and exciting themes for the perfect bridge to chapter books.

I Can Read! books have introduced children to the joy of reading since 1957. Featuring award-winning authors and illustrators and a fabulous cast of beloved characters, I Can Read! books set the standard for beginning readers.

A lifetime of discovery begins with the magical words **"I Can Read!"**

Visit www.icanread.com for information on enriching your child's reading experience.
Visit www.zonderkidz.com for more Zonderkidz I Can Read! titles.

Because your love is faithful, you will lead
the people you have set free. Because you
are so strong, you will guide them to the
holy place where you live.
—Exodus 15:12-14

ZONDERKIDZ

Moses, God's Brave Servant

Copyright © 2010 by Zondervan
Illustrations © 2010 by Dennis G. Jones

Requests for information should be addressed to:

Zonderkidz, *Grand Rapids, Michigan 49530*

Library of Congress Cataloging-in-Publication Data
Moses, God's Brave Servant / pictures by Dennis G. Jones
        p. cm. — (I can read!) (Dennis Jones series)
    ISBN 978-0-310-71882-6 (softcover)
        1. Moses (Biblical leader)—Juvenile literature. I. Jones, Dennis G., 1956-
BS580.M6G53 2010
222'.1209505—dc22   2009004155

Published in association with the literary agency of Alive Communica-
tions, Inc., 7680 Goddard Street #200, Colorado Springs, CO 80920.
www.alivecommunications.com

Zonderkidz is a trademark of Zondervan.

Editor: Mary Hassinger
Art direction: Sarah Molegraaf

Printed in China

10 11 12 13 /SCC/ 5 4 3 2 1

ZONDER**kidz**

MOSES
God's Brave Servant

pictures by Dennis G. Jones

Miriam was hiding.

Her baby brother was floating

in a basket.

Miriam's family was keeping

the baby safe from the king of Egypt.

The king didn't like Hebrew babies.

The king's daughter came

to the river.

She saw the baby in the basket.

She wanted to keep the baby safe too.

The princess took the baby

to the king's house.

She named the baby Moses.

Moses became her son.

The king didn't hurt Moses.

He grew up in the king's house.

Moses was a prince in Egypt.

When Moses was grown up,

he saw the Hebrews were slaves.

The Egyptians yelled at the slaves.

They made the slaves work hard.

Moses left Egypt.

He didn't like the way

the Egyptians treated the slaves.

Moses went to the wilderness

and took care of sheep.

One day, Moses saw a bush burning.

The bush never burned down!

God was in the bush.

God said, "Moses, tell the Egyptians
to let the slaves go."

Moses walked to Egypt.

He said to the king,

"God wants you to let the slaves go."

The king said no.

Moses told the king that

God would send plagues.

Plagues are very bad things.

The plagues would happen until

the king let the slaves go.

The river turned to blood.

Frogs and flies were everywhere.

Animals died. People got sick.

Hail hurt people. Bugs ate the food.

It was very dark for awhile too.

The last plague was the worst.

The king's son died.

Finally, the king let the slaves go.

Moses and the slaves packed up.

They walked out of Egypt.

The Hebrew slaves were free!

Moses and the Hebrews stopped.

The Red Sea was in front of them.

They couldn't cross the water.

The king changed his mind.

The king and his army were coming!

The Hebrews were trapped.

God had a plan to help the Hebrews.

He told Moses to raise his staff.

God would make a miracle happen.

When Moses raised his staff,

the water split in two.

The Hebrews could cross the Red Sea.

The Hebrews were amazed!

The Hebrews ran across the sea.

The king and his army followed.

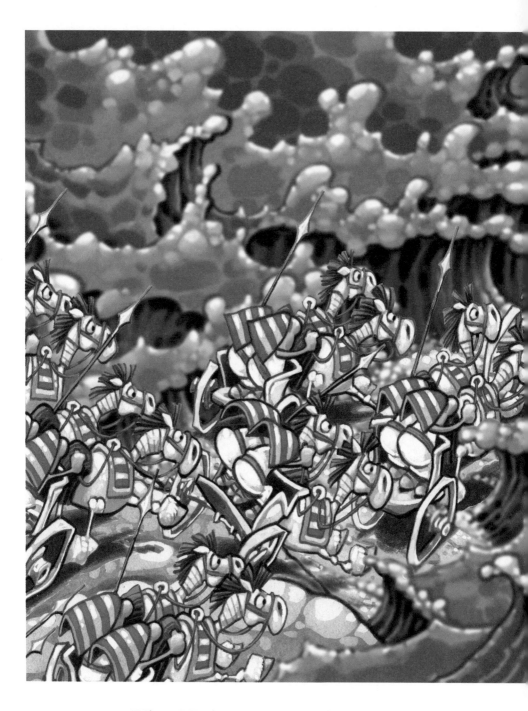

The Hebrews ran faster.

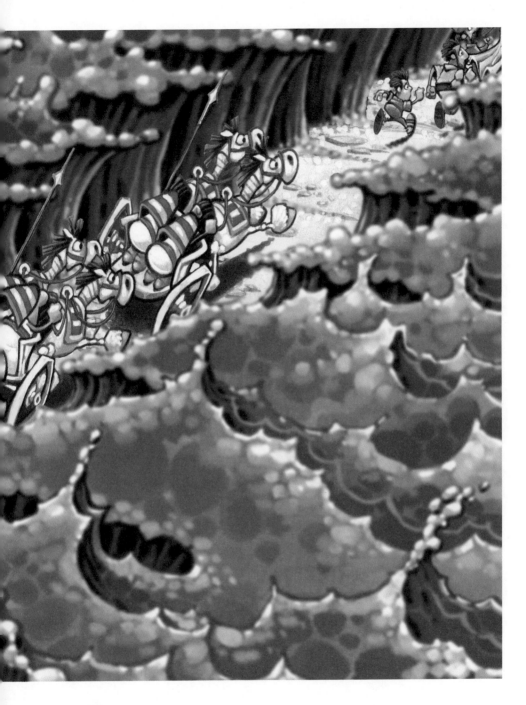

The king's army was getting closer.

When the last slave got across,

the water started to fall back down.

The king and his army

were still in the middle of the sea.

The horses were fast.

The army tried to get across.

The horses were not fast enough.

The water fell down.

The king and his army were stuck.

No Egyptians got to dry land.

All the Hebrews sang songs to God.

They danced and were happy.

God had saved his people!